THE RUGBY PUZZLE BOOK

THE RUGBY PUZZLE BOOK

Copyright © Summersdale Publishers Ltd, 2023

All rights reserved.

Text by Joe Varley

No part of this book may be reproduced by any means, nor transmitted, nor translated into a machine language, without the written permission of the publishers.

Condition of Sale
This book is sold subject to the condition that it shall not, by way of trade or otherwise, be lent, resold, hired out or otherwise circulated in any form of binding or cover other than that in which it is published and without a similar condition including this condition being imposed on the subsequent purchaser.

An Hachette UK Company
www.hachette.co.uk

Summersdale Publishers Ltd
Part of Octopus Publishing Group Limited
Carmelite House
50 Victoria Embankment
LONDON
EC4Y 0DZ
UK

www.summersdale.com

Printed and bound in CPI Group (UK) Ltd, Croydon, CR0 4YY

ISBN: 978-1-80007-922-9

Substantial discounts on bulk quantities of Summersdale books are available to corporations, professional associations and other organizations. For details contact general enquiries: telephone: +44 (0) 1243 771107 or email: enquiries@summersdale.com.

DISCLAIMER
All information featured in this book was correct at time of print. The author and publishers cannot accept responsibility for any inaccuracies and apologize in advance for any inadvertent errors in reporting.

THE RUGBY PUZZLE BOOK

BRAIN-TEASING PUZZLES, GAMES AND TRIVIA FOR RUGBY FANS

summersdale

INTRODUCTION

Attention all "rugger" fans!

The Rugby Puzzle Book will separate the real rugby brains from the casual observers with a superb selection of perplexing puzzles and tantalizing trivia. Included in this indispensable gift for players, coaches and fans are fiendish "what happened next?" scenarios, "strange but true" anecdotes, pub quiz-perfect stats and a whole host of crosswords, anagrams, general quizzes, and so much more!

Rugby was once described as "a game for barbarians played by gentlemen", but it's been played competitively by women, disabled athletes and some not-so-gentle men all around the globe for decades. Covering both Union and League formats, this book will keep readers of all ages entertained for the full 80 minutes – and even in the team bath afterwards!

So sit back in your favourite armchair and get stuck into a book covering famous players and unusual accounts of the much-loved sport played with a ball reputed to have originated from a pig's bladder!

TRIVIA
SACRÉ BLEU!

Following accusations of French foul play against Scotland in 1995, French coach Pierre Berbizier remarked, "If you can't take a punch, you should…"

a) Go to the ballet

b) Play table tennis

c) Practise boxing

WORD SEARCH

FAMOUS RUGBY CITIES

R	R	B	P	E	R	P	I	G	N	A	N
E	T	A	T	P	W	B	D	B	H	J	W
T	A	L	U	J	T	Y	Z	G	Z	M	Y
S	L	I	T	C	Y	P	R	Q	V	Z	M
E	O	T	R	N	K	U	N	L	P	F	J
C	N	N	K	O	B	L	S	B	F	J	L
U	D	G	R	N	T	Y	A	I	K	Y	K
O	O	Q	I	B	D	E	D	N	N	P	Q
L	N	D	J	N	M	R	R	Z	D	L	X
G	E	Y	E	L	A	T	M	P	T	G	J
Y	M	Y	B	C	T	G	M	B	M	Y	T

Auckland, Cardiff, Sydney, Pretoria, London,
Perpignan, Gloucester, Edinburgh

CROSSWORD

RUGBY TERMS

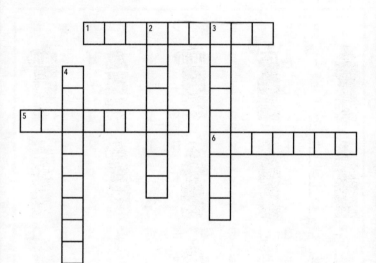

ACROSS
1 Play immediately after a tackle, car not working (9)
5 Conceding possession, small pie (apple?) (8)
6 Position, 50% of an insect (3,4)

DOWN
2 Tackle, pat above the foot (5,3)
3 Ball goes straight out (2,3,4)
4 Also known as an "up and under" (9)

PAIRS GAME

Match up the 20 water bottles in 20 seconds. The first one has been done for you.

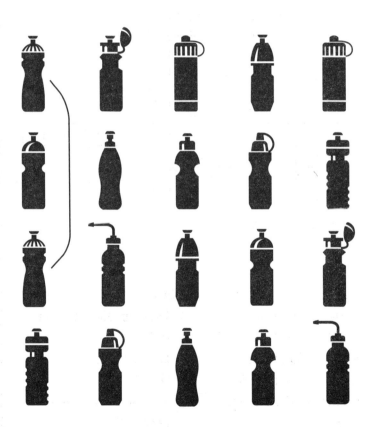

TRIVIA
GIMME FIVE!

1. As of 2022, who is the highest points scorer in rugby Test matches?

2. The Calcutta Cup is contested between which two countries?

3. As of 2022, which club has won the Heineken Cup the most times?

4. What is the nickname of the Argentine men's rugby union team?

5. Australian Nick Farr-Jones primarily played in what position?

WORD WHEEL

See how many words of four or more letters you can make from the letters below. All words must include the central letter, and proper nouns don't count! Can you find the surname of a New Zealand rugby player that uses all the letters? He's played over 100 times for the Kiwis!

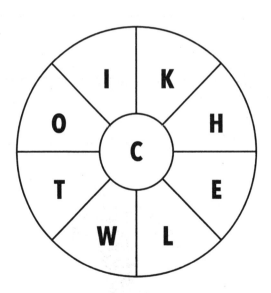

MAZE

Can you help legendary rugby referee Nigel Owens find his whistle?

ANAGRAMS
RED ROSES

The following four female England rugby union players are in anagram form. Work out who the players are - they were all named in the 2022 squad.

EVIL A DARKS

NIL DUKE NELLIE

HER SOAR ZION

RAE RICK MAPLE

TRIVIA
JAPANESE STYLE

Japan were proud hosts of the 2019 Rugby World Cup. As Japan is a nation steeped in tradition, players from other nations were asked to cover up their tattoos in public – particularly the New Zealand players, who are famous for their body art. Why are tattoos deemed undesirable in public in Japan?

a) Historically, Shinto shuns any form of tattoos because Raijin, the god of thunder and storms, favoured body art and he is considered bad fortune.

b) Tattoos are banned in depictions of traditional Ukiyo-e art, which led to Emperor Naruhito prohibiting any form of tattoos in public during the duration of the tournament.

c) Tattoos are associated with the yakuza – Japan's network of crime syndicates.

WORD LADDER

In this word ladder, change one letter at a time to turn the word BROW into PROP.

BROW
____
____
____
____
PROP

RIDDLE

A common skill in rugby is the answer to this riddle.

My first is in drop kick but not in penalty
My second is in ruck but not in recycle
My third is in maul but not in touchline
My fourth is in Pumas but not in Springboks
My fifth is in try but not in drive

What am I?

DOT-TO-DOT

Join the dots to find the mystery image!

TRIVIA
ALL IN A ROE

In 1982 during an England vs. Australia rugby match, a lady named Erika Roe became famous for her half-time antics. How did the 24-year-old achieve rugby fame?

a) She smuggled a trumpet into Twickenham stadium and led the 60,000-strong crowd into a stirring rendition of "Swing Low, Sweet Chariot".

b) She "bared all" as one of the most famous streakers in sport and was led off the pitch by bemused – but amused – officials.

c) She snuck into the Australian changing room, posing as a member of the media crew to help her career. Australian player Brendan Moon answered all her questions, even though she didn't have any ID or microphone!

SPOT THE DIFFERENCE

Can you find the 10 differences between these two pictures?

REBUS

Can you work out what is suggested by the diagrams below? To give you a helping hand we'll give you a clue: 11 February 2007.

MISSING VOWELS

Here are the names of some famous England male rugby union players – past and present – with the vowels deleted. Can you work out the names? Steady on – they get harder!

JNNY WLKNSN

MRTN JHNSN

BRN MR

BLL BMNT

WLL CRLNG

JSN LNRD

RB NDRW

LLS GNG

MK VNPL

J CKNSG

TRIVIA
WORLD RANKINGS

In early November 2022, World Rugby updated the rugby union ratings for all participating countries for both the men's and women's teams. Two teams have been deleted from each list – can you name the four missing countries?

MEN'S

Rank	Country	Points
1	Ireland	90.63
2	France	89.41
3	New Zealand	88.64
4	South Africa	88.41
5	England	84.45
6	?	83.01
7	Australia	82.02
8	Scotland	80.74
9	Wales	80.28
10	?	77.39

WOMEN'S

Rank	Country	Points
1	England	96.78
2	New Zealand	89.57
3	?	87.83
4	France	86.09
5	Italy	79.82
6	Australia	78.00
7	?	76.78
8	Ireland	74.01
9	Wales	72.70
10	Scotland	68.71

COUNTING CONUNDRUM

$+$ $= 16$

$+$ $= 11$

$+$ $= 13$

$+$ $= ?$

CROSSWORD

ENGLISH CLUB NICKNAMES

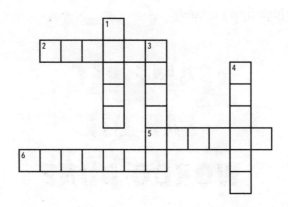

ACROSS
2 Leaders of a clan (6)
5 Largest cats (6)
6 High-flying birds of prey (7)

DOWN
1 Chicago American Football team (5)
3 E.g. Patrick, David, George, etc. (6)
4 Large cartilaginous fish (plural) (6)

ANAGRAMS
WINGING IT

Rearrange these letters to reveal the surnames of famous rugby union high-flying wingers:

SAME PEC

SAR OIL

WORDO DUNE

HELT TOW

TRIVIA
MEN'S 11–20 NATIONS

World Rugby's rankings alter from season to season. From the start of November 2022, here is a list of the nations of the men's game that fill the 11–20 spot. However, two nations have been missed out – which two?

Rank	Nation
11	Samoa
12	Fiji
13	Georgia
14	Italy
15	?
16	Tonga
17	Romania
18	Uruguay
19	USA
20	?

RIDDLE

Get your rugby brain into gear to solve this riddle!

My first is in Saracens but not in Argentina
My second is Pienaar but not in Wilkinson
My third is in van der Westhuizen but not in Gregan
My fourth is in Evans but not in Hastings
My fifth is in Northampton but not in Leeds
My sixth is in Hansen but not in Woodward

What am I?

WORD WHEEL

See how many words of four or more letters you can make from
the letters below, using each letter just once. All words must use
the central letter. Can you find the nickname of a rugby union
team that uses all the letters?

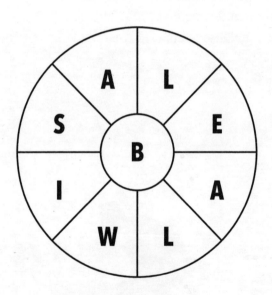

DOT-TO-DOT

Join the dots to find the mystery image!

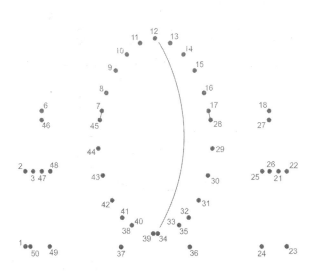

SPOT THE DIFFERENCE

Can you find the 10 differences between these two pictures?

MISSING LETTERS

Below are ten men's rugby union nations that, as of October 2022, are ranked 21-30 in the world. However, most of their letters have been deleted, including all the first letters. How many nations can you name?

Rank	Nation
21	HIL
22	NG ON
23	ANAA
24	AMIA
25	USA
26	EGIU
27	RAIL
28	ETHELNS
29	OLAN
30	EMAN

PAIRS GAME

Match up the 20 sport socks in 20 seconds. The first one has been done for you.

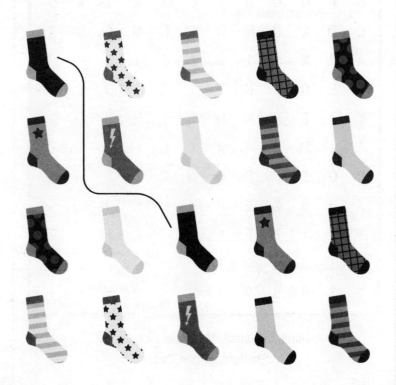

WORD SEARCH

KIWI UNION GREATS

D	F	O	U	A	K	C	A	R	I	K	D
C	O	L	U	M	O	L	B	V	C	O	R
A	B	N	O	I	R	Z	A	I	N	U	O
R	S	D	T	H	U	I	R	K	J	O	F
T	Z	E	Y	N	O	T	T	H	O	B	L
E	I	M	E	W	A	C	C	M	N	I	E
R	O	S	K	P	O	W	F	D	E	M	H
A	R	G	Z	E	R	T	R	Z	S	K	S
P	I	T	E	F	K	L	O	I	Z	U	R
L	I	V	R	O	I	B	L	O	K	J	M
F	T	B	V	R	S	D	A	E	M	I	T

Lomu, Fitzpatrick, Meads, McCaw, Jones,
Shelford, Kirwan, Carter

DONALD'S LATE CALL-UP

When New Zealand needed a replacement fly-half for their 2011 Rugby Union World Cup final match, they called-up Stephen Donald. However, it didn't quite go to plan. Why was this?

a) Donald had "officially" retired from rugby and was enjoying his down-time when he bumped into a news reporter on Auckland's Queen Street. She relayed the number of injuries that had befallen the All Blacks, so Donald emailed the coaching staff and asked "as a joke" if he could help them out. And help them out he did!

b) Donald was the All Black's fourth-choice fly-half. He'd taken a fishing trip on the Waikato River, and the coaching staff were initially unable to contact him. Kiwi player Mils Muliaina eventually got through to Donald's mobile phone, yelling "Answer your phone, you idiot!" (or words to that effect!).

c) Donald was babysitting his niece the day before the final. He was unsure whether to play when asked, but his niece said that if her uncle didn't, she'd start crying and wouldn't stop until the end of the final. That'd be enough of an incentive to play!

LETTERBOX

Some of the letters below occur more than once. Cross them out and the remaining letters will then spell out a well-known rugby club. What is it?

N	D	A	O	F
R	U	P	S	C
W	E	V	O	F
T	S	W	D	H
M	U	R	N	M
V	E	B	P	C

WORD LADDER

In this word ladder, change one letter at a time to turn the word MELT into BALL.

MELT

_ _ _ _

_ _ _ _

_ _ _ _

_ _ _ _

BALL

MAZE

Most of the great rugby kickers need a kicking tee to help them guide the ball over the posts. Can you find a route through the maze so the ball finds its way to the kicking tee?

TRIVIA
QUOTE COMPLETIONS

The following are rugby quotations but with some words missing. What did the following people say?

1. After a quarter final victory over Australia, Number 8 star Nick Easter had these acerbic words for the media: "I'd like to thank the press…"
a) for their unflinching unprofessionalism
b) from the heart of my bottom
c) on behalf of Rupert Murdoch

2. American footballer Joe Theismann was the NFL's Most Valuable Player in 1983. Who better to give us an opinion of rugby from "across the pond"? He once said, "Rugby is great. The players don't wear helmets or padding; they just beat the living daylights out of each other and then…"
a) go for a beer
b) shake hands
c) do it again the next week

RUGBY JUMBLE

A handful of rugby terms have been separated and jumbled up. Your job is to find the four terms used in the world of rugby by joining them up again.

OF	ON	BLO
ASH	FLO	ODB
CON	BALL	AD
VERSI	CR	IN

REBUS

Can you work out what is suggested by the diagrams below?
It's a well-known team.

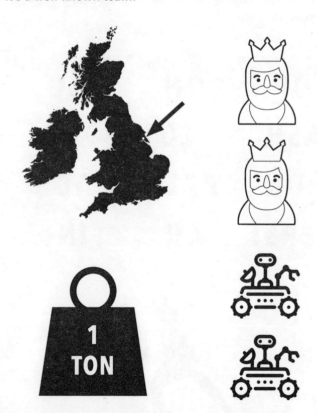

DOT-TO-DOT

Join the dots to find the mystery image!

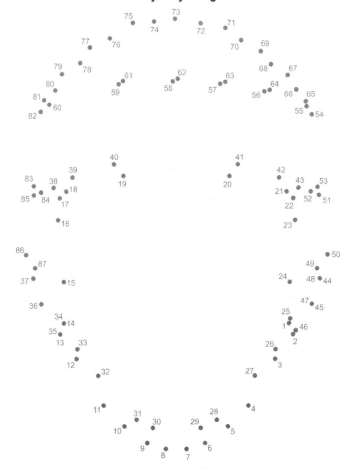

TRIVIA
STRANGE BUT TRUE

Siddal Rugby Club in Halifax, West Yorkshire, has an interesting history – one which will delight legions of rugby fans. Which one of the following "facts" about the Yorkshire club is true?

a) The club was owned by the notorious gangster Charles Sabini, who only permitted spectators entry when they gave the club's stewards a password. The special code words changed every game, and because followers of the club couldn't remember them, the club disbanded after just five months.

b) The club's site was once the location of Halifax Zoo. The attraction received a royal visit from King George V, but ultimately the zoo had to close due to reports of animal abuse, animal attacks on the public and even escapes by dangerous creatures, including boars, elephants and bears.

c) Because of Halifax's wealth from the cotton and wool industry, the club could afford West Yorkshire's first ever legal "gentleman's club". It lasted until disapproving neighbours complained to authorities about the less than wholesome night-time activities.

ANAGRAMS
WHISTLEBLOWERS

Rearrange these letters to reveal notable rugby referees.

DEAR CAN ELLIS

NAN YEW BEARS

CAP JOY PEER

PEAK CU REEL

WORD WHEEL

See how many words of four or more letters you can make from the letters below, using each letter just once. All words must use the central letter. Can you find the name of a famous rugby league city that uses all the letters?

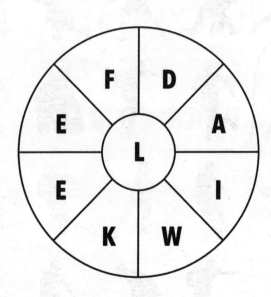

PAIRS GAME

Match up the 20 rugby players in 20 seconds. The first one has been done for you.

TRIVIA
GETTING QUIZZICAL

Puzzles are great, but let's get back to basics with this short rugby quiz.

1. As of November 2022, who is Italy's leading points scorer in rugby union internationals?

2. What was the name of the 2005 US documentary film about wheelchair rugby players?

3. The crossbar on the goalposts in league and union is how many metres above the ground?

4. As of November 2022, who is Ireland's top try scorer in rugby union history?

5. Florin Vlaicu is a points machine in rugby union. For what nation did he win his first cap in 2006?

6. In which city is Newlands Stadium?

7. Who was the head coach of the England rugby union side from 2006–2008?

8. For which country does Theresa Fitzpatrick play?

WORD SEARCH

ENGLISH WOMEN'S PLAYERS

O	K	I	D	T	I	N	F	U	T	E
K	I	B	H	T	W	O	A	N	H	L
C	L	A	W	A	B	A	M	A	O	T
T	D	I	B	R	I	L	R	I	M	E
B	U	D	E	A	T	R	H	D	P	N
S	N	V	J	C	I	A	M	N	S	Y
A	N	W	E	S	G	H	W	I	O	A
W	E	S	O	I	O	V	B	W	N	K
E	T	N	A	F	N	I	E	T	K	O
H	A	R	S	E	I	V	A	D	L	C

Scarratt, Cokayne, Infante, Thompson, Kildunne,
Harrison, Ward, Davies

47

LETTER GRID

Rugby brains at the ready! The following seven cities or towns have all been venues for World Cup rugby union matches – but they are each missing one letter. Find the missing letter and place it in the grid below to spell out something that frustrates players, fans and coaches! What's the word?

1. AUC_LAND
2. GRE_OBLE
3. STELLENB_SCH
4. LAUN_ESTON
5. FU_UROI
6. G_SFORD
7. BAYO_NE

1	2	3	4	5	6	7

TRIVIA:
2003 RUGBY UNION WORLD CUP FINAL

How's your memory? Below are the starting line-ups for the famous 2003 World Cup final, which took place in Sydney in November of that year. We've left out three players on each team – can you recall their names?

Shirt number	Australian player	Shirt number	English player
15	Mat Rogers	15	?
14	Wendell Sailor	14	Jason Robinson
13	?	13	Will Greenwood
12	Elton Flatley	12	?
11	Lote Tuqiri	11	Ben Cohen
10	?	10	Jonny Wilkinson
9	George Gregan (c)	9	Matt Dawson
8	David Lyons	8	Lawrence Dallaglio
7	Phil Waugh	7	?
6	?	6	Richard Hill
5	Nathan Sharpe	5	Ben Kay
4	Justin Harrison	4	Martin Johnson (c)
3	Al Baxter	3	Phil Vickery
2	Brendan Cannon	2	Steve Thompson
1	Bill Young	1	Trevor Woodman

TRIVIA
PNG

Rugby league is by far the most popular sport in Papua New Guinea, with thousands of fans rushing to the nearest TV whenever their beloved national team is playing. They are known as "The Kumuls", and their nickname is often cited by commentators. But what is a "kumul"?

a) A series of warships historically harboured in the country's capital, Port Moresby.

b) Any of the elaborate symbols adopted by the Evangelical Lutheran Church of Papua New Guinea, which represents a significant proportion of the country.

c) It means bird-of-paradise in a widely used language in Papua New Guinea.

MISSING VOWELS

The following UK northern rugby league stadiums have had
their vowels removed. No, it's not a medical operation – just a
fiendish puzzle! With plenty of stadiums changing their names
for various reasons, scoring a "perfect ten" will be quite an
achievement – especially considering the last one is vowel-free!

BLL V _ _ _ _ _ _ _ _

HDNGLY _ _ _ _ _ _ _ _ _ _

DSL _ _ _ _ _

TTLLY WCKD _ _ _ _ _ _ _ _ _ _ _ _ _

CRVN PRK _ _ _ _ _ _ _ _ _ _

HLLWLL JNS _ _ _ _ _ _ _ _ _ _ _ _ _ _

JHN SMTH'S _ _ _ _ _ _ _ _ _ _

KNGSTN PRK _ _ _ _ _ _ _ _ _ _ _ _

CGR PRK _ _ _ _ _ _ _ _ _ _

_ _ [STADIUM]

LETTERBOX

Cross out all the letters below that appear more than once. The remaining letters will then spell out a legendary retired rugby league player. Can you work out his identity?

B	D	S	U	Y
R	I	H	M	C
L	W	C	S	T
R	F	W	F	E
T	I	B	U	G
N	M	A	G	D

MAZE

Whether injured or simply just cold, some rugby players consider heat spray as an essential addition to the medical kit bag. In this maze, can you find a route for the heat spray to make its way to the medical bag?

TRIVIA
STRANGE BUT TRUE

As the title suggests, this rugby head-scratcher is a little on the bizarre side. One of the three statements below about Thomas Gisborne Gordon (born in 1851) is true. Can you identify the correct statement about the North of Ireland FC and Ireland international?

a) Gisborne first played for Ireland in 1877, and he has the distinction of being the only one-handed international rugby player.

b) While Gisborne's rugby skills were undisputed, his first call-up for his country in 1883 was the result of him becoming substituted at a nearby football match; the Ireland rugby team required a player to replace an injured hooker and Gisborne was the only available sportsman.

c) As a staunch supporter of the working classes, Gisborne refused to play without his beloved bowler hat, manufactured by the London company Lock & Co. Hatters.

RUGBY JUMBLE

Some famous Welsh surnames of male rugby union players have been split and jumbled up. Simply find the four surnames by joining them up again. When we say "simply", that's a matter of opinion!

RDS   NO   PUR

AU   ED   TI

IC   LET   WA

RTH   FA

SPOT THE DIFFERENCE

Can you find the 10 differences between these two pictures?

CROSSWORD

RUGBY PLAYERS

ACROSS

3 Argentine hooker, Julián ___ (7)

5 Scottish fly-half, Finn ___ (7)

6 South African winger, Cheslin ___ (5)

DOWN

1 England Women's captain, Sarah ___ (6)

2 Kiwi brothers (7)

4 English player, 1997–2003, Austin ___ (6)

TRIVIA
CHEIK MATE!

In November 2022, rugby coach Michael Cheika was dubbed "possibly the busiest man in world rugby" by a major British newspaper. Why?

a) Cheika boarded a plane to Papua New Guinea just 30 minutes after attending five consecutive press conferences – on the same day as his wedding! How busy can you be?

b) He coached the Lebanese rugby league side against his native Australia, then oversaw the Argentine rugby union side when they came up against England two days later. Coaching two national rugby teams in different formats just 48 hours apart – now that is busy!

c) He signed a new coaching contract on the same day as he launched his new sporting management company. At least he didn't forget to read the small print!

WORD SEARCH

SUPER RUGBY TEAMS

H	W	E	S	K	I	V	E	C	R	O
J	U	A	C	B	R	E	B	E	L	S
L	E	R	T	R	V	K	W	A	R	E
V	U	I	R	T	O	N	G	R	O	I
B	L	C	H	I	E	F	S	E	R	B
U	I	D	S	W	C	F	C	D	R	M
S	H	A	T	A	R	A	W	S	E	U
W	I	O	B	F	I	N	N	G	O	R
B	L	U	E	S	H	L	I	E	K	B
R	O	I	W	B	F	C	H	R	S	I

Reds, Hurricanes, Rebels, Brumbies,
Waratahs, Blues, Force, Chiefs

WORD LADDER

In this word ladder, change one letter at a time to turn the word
BOOT into RUCK.

BOOT

_ _ _ _

_ _ _ _

_ _ _ _

_ _ _ _

RUCK

REBUS

Time for another picture puzzle! Can you work out what is suggested by the diagrams below? It's something familiar to a lot of rugby players.

TRIVIA
FIVE NATIONS TROPHY

The designs of many awards and trophies have developed over time, and the Five Nations trophy is no different. Nowadays, the competition is called the Six Nations Championship (for obvious reasons), but the trophy itself has evolved to reflect modern times. However, which of the following statements is true regarding the Five Nations Championship trophy?

a) It was designed by Queen Victoria, who was a fan of most sports. In fact, prior to her death in 1901, it was suggested that her image be engraved on the base of the trophy, so every time it was raised by the victor, they'd see her beaming face!

b) The trophy was originally designed using malleable pulp made from French cypress trees. Once a crude model was sculpted from the pulp, it was transformed to its basic glory by manufacturers Fattorini Ltd.

c) Its capacity was 3.75 litres – the equivalent of five bottles of champagne, or one bottle for each of the original nations.

DOT-TO-DOT

Join the dots to find the mystery image!

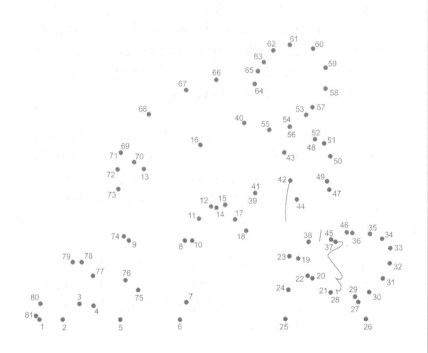

REBUS

Work out the rugby term from the following picture clues.

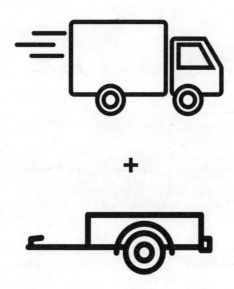

PAIRS GAME

Match up the 20 rugby boots in 20 seconds. The first one has been done for you.

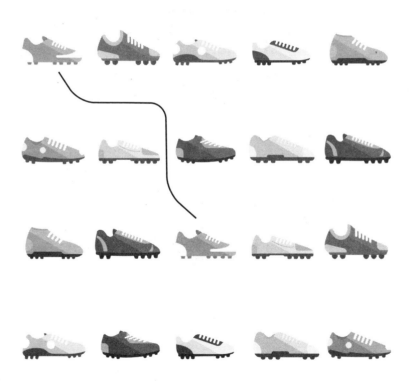

TRIVIA
SORRY, NOT ME, BOSS!

Before the England rugby union squad headed out to South Africa for the 1995 World Cup, head coach Jack Rowell discovered a player had snuck in at 2 a.m., prompting an alcohol ban. Rowell accused Jason Leonard of a breach of protocol at the training session the following day. The legendary prop forward flatly denied it – why?

a) Leonard was on the wagon to win a £500 bet with colleague Brian Moore

b) The thirsty Englishman had to go home extra early because he fell over in a pub in the afternoon!

c) As Leonard admitted to fellow forward Martin Bayfield, "It couldn't have been me – I didn't get in until 4 a.m.!"

WORD WHEEL

See how many words of four or more letters you can make from the letters below, using each letter just once – no cheating, please, or you'll be sin-binned! All words must use the central letter. Can you find the name of something that is essential for all rugby matches?

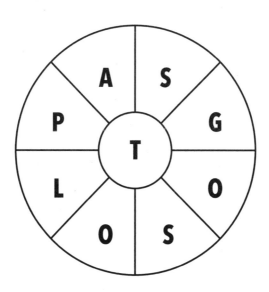

ANAGRAMS
STADIUMS

Rearrange these letters to reveal some well-known rugby stadiums. You might even have been to some of them, and they've all hosted many exciting Test matches!

FUR DREAMILY

DEEP RANK

KITCHEN WAM

SPIRAL ELK

RIDDLE

The surname of an Australian forward is the answer to this riddle.

My first is in half time but not in full time
My second is in box kick but not in advantage
My third is in blood bin but not in crash ball
My fourth is in Pontypool but not in Neath
My fifth is in Leicester but not in Wasps
My sixth is in back row but not in blind side

Who am I?

FUN FACTS

Preston Grasshoppers is one of the most famous and oldest rugby clubs in the world. Here's a little bit of trivia about the club's history to amaze your friends in the clubhouse.

At the Bull Hotel in Preston, Lancashire, a meeting was held on 28 September 1869, where it was declared: "That a club be at once formed in Preston to play football with the Rugby Rules of the game but without hacking. That the club be called 'The Preston Grasshoppers'."

The nickname "Grasshoppers" was chosen by founders who were several old boys of Cheltenham College, and later arranged a first game where the "Fireflies" played against the "Grasshoppers". Once the Rugby Football Union was formed, the Grasshoppers adopted the official laws of the game, which officially outlawed "Hacking" and "Tripping". "Hacking" is best described as where anyone lying in a ruck was fair game and could be kicked below the knee until they wisely got out of harm's way!

Players associated with Preston Grasshoppers include: England second-row Wade Dooley, rugby league great Sean Long, back John Kirkpatrick, and Yorkshireman Graham Holroyd.

WORD SEARCH

RUGBY ACCESSORIES

A	D	E	S	T	O	O	B	O	R	T
T	R	H	E	A	T	S	P	R	A	Y
B	A	R	C	A	T	V	I	C	L	O
S	U	Y	B	T	U	I	K	E	P	S
O	G	I	V	B	I	L	V	C	E	T
C	H	T	A	P	E	R	A	W	O	R
K	T	I	L	P	W	M	Y	I	Y	O
B	U	P	A	C	M	U	R	C	S	H
R	O	D	L	U	W	P	T	B	J	S
I	M	C	Y	E	S	R	E	J	O	B

Boots, Mouth Guard, Heat Spray, Jersey, Shorts,
Tape, Scrum Cap, Tackle Pad

RUGBY JUMBLE

The names of four cups or trophies contested for in the world of rugby have been separated and jumbled up. To claim the puzzle trophy, reassemble the sections of letters to find their names. The words "cup" or "trophy" have been omitted.

TTA	**DOW**	**ISL**
LIS	**NE**	**OE**
BB	**NS**	**CA**
BL	**LCU**	**EL**
ED	**LA**	**WE**

SPOT THE DIFFERENCE

Can you find the 10 differences between these two pictures?

TRIVIA
TRICOLORE (SUR)PRIZE!

Formidable French forward Benoît Dauga was one of Les Blues' greatest players, having earned 63 caps in the 1960s and 70s. Sadly he passed away in 2022. Dauga won three Five Nations championships with France and was the archetypical brawny rugby player on the pitch – but a gentleman off it. When he was awarded the Prix de la Gauloise, what did he receive?

a) A lifetime supply of camembert cheese. As a farmer, Dauga requested his prize after receiving notification from the French rugby board, and promptly organized a five-course dinner with his playing pals as way of a celebration – with the camembert featuring heavily on the cheeseboard!

b) His weight in Cognac. Dauga weighed roughly 100 kg, so a quick calculation reveals that the volume of the intoxicating French liquor would have been about 100 litre bottles. Imagine the hangover!

c) Away from the rugby pitch, Dauga was a keen hunter in and around the forests of his native Pyrenees. To honour his hobby, he was rewarded with two top-of-the-range hunting rifles.

MAZE

In this maze, can you help the rugby player find their way to the bar for a well-earned drink?

RIDDLE

A rugby league legend is the answer to this riddle.

My first is in South Africa but not in Ireland
My second is in Fiji but not in Samoa
My third is in France but not in Scotland
My fourth is in Papua New Guinea but not in Wales
My fifth is in New Zealand but not in Belgium
My sixth is in Hong Kong but not in Georgia

Who am I?

CROSSWORD

NON-BRITISH RUGBY, PAST OR PRESENT

ACROSS

4 Destructive in a china shop (5)

6 Based in Dunedin (11)

DOWN

1 Fast land mammals (8)

2 French city famous for sausages and cassoulets (8)

3 11–13th century military voyagers (9)

5 Oldest rugby club in Italy, founded in Rome (5)

TRIVIA
STADIUMS AROUND THE WORLD

Can you name the location where these rugby stadiums are to be found?

1. Kings Park Stadium
a) Durban,
South Africa

b) Christchurch,
New Zealand

c) Brisbane,
Australia

2. The Sevens
a) Singapore

b) Dubai

c) Hong Kong

3. Jose Amalfitani Stadium
a) Santiago,
Chile

b) Buenos Aires,
Argentina

c) Milan,
Italy

4. Stadio Flaminio
a) Lisbon,
Portugal

b) Montevideo,
Uruguay

c) Rome,
Italy

FOLLOW THE LETTERS

To solve this puzzle, start with the circled letter. Moving one letter at a time, either vertically or horizontally, find four surnames of rugby players, past or present. They've all gained at least 50 caps for their country.

J	O	H	T	R	O	I
I	E	N	S	E	W	F
K	D	T	O	R	G	S
C	L	O	N	D	N	H
B	L	N	T	T	A	O
O	A	U	M	A	G	E
E	E	L	C	B	R	S

MISSING VOWELS

In July 2022, a well-known sports broadcasting company confirmed the full list of their rugby presenters and pundits for the summer rugby union internationals, which featured England, Ireland, Scotland and Wales. Some of the presenters and pundit's names are below – minus the vowels. Can you work out the names?

SRR LGN

JNTHN DVS

MGG LPHNS

DYLN HRTLY

STRT HGG

SN FTZPTRCK

MCHL LYNGH

BRYN HBN

LN QNLN

JM RBRTS

WORD LADDER

In this word ladder, change one letter at a time to turn the word POPE into MAUL.

POPE
_ _ _ _
_ _ _ _
_ _ _ _
_ _ _ _
MAUL

TRIVIA
SIX NATIONS SING-A-LONG

Below are multiple choice questions about some of the national anthems sung by Six Nations rugby teams. How many can you correctly identify?

1. "God Save The King/Queen" is one of the most famous national anthems. Which country's national anthem is set to its melody?

a) Belgium   b) Liechtenstein   c) Andorra

1. In 2006, a poll of 10,000 Scots revealed what percentage of those locals chose "Flower of Scotland" as their preferred national anthem?

a) 41%   b) 62%   c) 83%

3. What was the original title of the French national anthem "La Marseillaise"?

a) "France Never Defeated"   b) "Napoleon's Legions March On"   c) "War Song for the Army of the Rhine"

LETTERBOX

Cross out all the letters below that appear more than once, and you'll be left with a rugby-playing nation. But which one?

E	B	M	S	R
K	C	V	L	D
I	P	T	V	I
H	T	F	K	O
S	L	B	P	D
H	N	M	O	A

REBUS

Can you work out what is suggested by the diagrams below? It's something that coaches and managers never want to see in a rugby match!

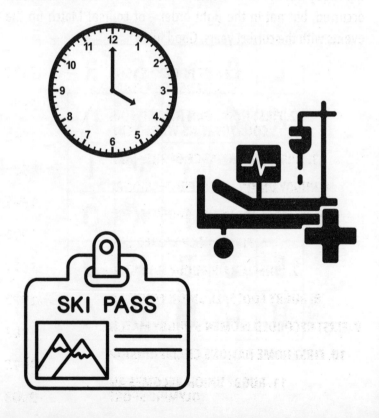

TRIVIA
RUGBY TIMELINE

Below are some momentous moments that have happened in the rugby world. We've included the years on which the events occurred, but not in the right order – of course! Match up the events with the correct years. Good luck!

1. FIRST RUGBY LEAGUE CHALLENGE CUP FINAL	**1871**
	1871
2. FIRST NORTHERN HEMISPHERE COUNTRY WINS WORLD CUP	
	1883
3. FIRST PERFORMANCE OF THE HAKA	
	1888
4. RUGBY UNION TURNS PROFESSIONAL	
5. FIRST INTERNATIONAL RUGBY MATCH	**1897**
6. FIRST RUGBY WORLD CUP	**1900**
7. WHEELCHAIR RUGBY INVENTED	**1917**
8. RUGBY FOOTBALL UNION FOUNDED	**1977**
9. FIRST RECORDED WOMEN'S RUGBY MATCH	**1987**
10. FIRST HOME NATIONS CHAMPIONSHIP	**1995**
11. RUGBY UNION BECOMES AN OLYMPIC SPORT	**2003**

WORD SEARCH

RUGBY LEAGUE POSITIONS

```
S  T  A  N  D  O  F  F  O  E  L
A  W  E  M  O  R  D  I  R  J  G
P  O  R  P  O  I  S  T  O  F  N
O  R  L  E  R  S  N  W  U  R  I
H  D  P  F  U  E  B  L  F  E  W
R  N  S  A  C  E  L  H  B  K  T
H  O  L  T  I  B  W  R  I  O  H
A  C  F  T  A  O  E  U  B  O  G
O  E  K  C  A  B  F  L  A  H  I
L  S  K  L  U  G  W  K  F  O  R
```

Hooker, Prop, Full Back, Left Centre, Right Wing,
Second Row, Stand Off, Half Back

PAIRS GAME

Match up the 20 shirts in 20 seconds. The first one has been done for you.

WORD WHEEL

It's Word Wheel time again! See how many words of four or more letters you can make from the below letters, using each letter just once. All words must use the central letter. Can you find the name of a rugby playing position that uses all nine letters?

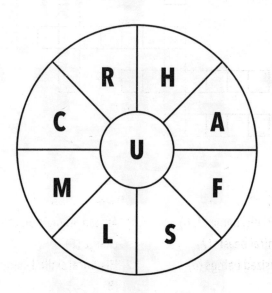

CROSSWORD

RUGBY LEAGUE NICKNAMES

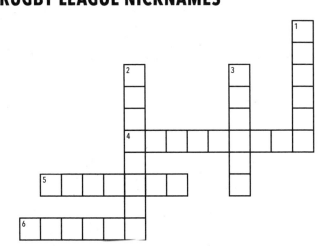

ACROSS

4 MUFC nickname (3, 6)
5 Mythical beasts (7)
6 Oversized beings (6)

DOWN

1 African animals on the charge (6)
2 Historical skilled soldiers (8)
3 They hunt in packs (6)

TRIVIA
RUGBY HISTORY

1. The first rugby union international, in 1871, was won by Scotland (2 tries, 1 goal) against England (1 try). What was the score?

a) 5–2   b) 7–3   c) 1–0

2. Fans like to see free-flowing rugby, so the IRFB (now World Rugby) decided to increase the value of a try in rugby union to five points. But in which year was the first 5 point international try scored?

a) 1995   b) 1992   c) 1990

3. To punish teams or players for deliberately preventing an easy try being scored, a penalty try worth seven points was adopted. In which year?

a) 2019   b) 2017   c) 2014

DOT-TO-DOT

Join the dots to find the mystery image! It's a nickname of a successful rugby league team.

SPOT THE DIFFERENCE

Can you find the 10 differences between these two pictures?

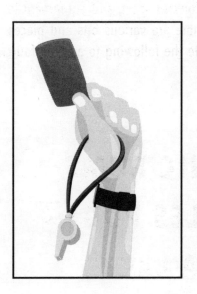 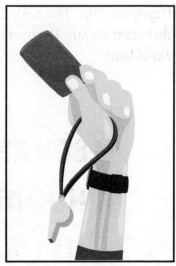

ANAGRAMS
RUGGER'S EQUIPMENT

Rugby is a relatively straightforward sport, and equipment is largely minimal. That said, there are various bits and pieces that assist players. Unscramble the following to achieve four-out-of-four!

MECHANIC RUMS

A HURDLES PODS

GET BA LACK

TEAR TOW BELT

TRIVIA
RUGBY WORDS

How well do you know rugby? Let's find out! What do the following words or phrases mean?

1. Short arm penalty
a) Any penalty awarded by the TMO (Television Match Official)
b) A penalty awarded for particularly dangerous play
c) Another name for a free kick

2. Shoeing
a) Colloquial term, derived from the 19th century, for studs on rugby boots
b) Time given by the referee to players replacing unfastened boots
c) Moving opposing players away from the ruck with their boots

3. Sipi Tau
a) New Zealand's strict rugby code of conduct
b) Tongan war dance performed before international matches
c) Name given to Fiji's national captain

RUGBY JUMBLE

The surnames of four male England rugby league players have been separated and jumbled up. The four names were all named in the England squad for the 2021 Rugby League World Cup (played in 2022, of course!). Can you find the four players by rejoining the groups of letters?

BA	BU	NS
NS	TKI	ESS
MA	TEM	ON
WA	RG	KI
	AN	

ODD ONE OUT

Which of the following rugby union player anagrams is the anomaly? You'll need a mixture of skills to work out the correct answer, so we wish you the best of luck with this one!

1. LU JAM HOON

2. DAC RANTER

3. JAR EEL ROM

4. MAT RHINO

5. HOL BOR YEW

6. MAIL WHALE SINS

7. NOC SEAL GREB

RIDDLE

A good rugby tactic in wet conditions is the answer to this riddle.

My first is in Diego Dominguez but not in Rory Underwood
My second is in Rory Underwood but not in Diego Dominguez
My third is in Jonah Lomu but not in Martin Johnson
My fourth is in Mike Gibson but not in Will Carling
My fifth is in Barry John but not in David Kirk
My sixth is in David Campese but not in Jonny Wilkinson
My seventh is in Lawrence Dallaglio but not in Michael Jones

What am I?

TRIVIA
FAIR PLAY OR FAKE?

Here are some "stats" about the thrilling world of wheelchair rugby. Can you select the true statements from the porky pies?

1. Wheelchair rugby originated in France. True or false?

2. The first World Championships took place in 1995 in Switzerland. True or false?

3. The two small wheels at the front of the wheelchair are known as "casters". True or false?

4. International rules state that any player can communicate with the officials on behalf of the coach or other players. True or false?

5. Once in possession of the ball, teams have 60 seconds to score a try. True or false?

6. Players are assessed and put into one of seven classes, from 0.5 to 3.5. True or false?

WORD LADDER

In this word ladder, change one letter at a time to turn the word LOFT into PASS.

LOFT

_ _ _ _

_ _ _ _

_ _ _ _

_ _ _ _

PASS

REBUS

Can you work out what is suggested by the diagrams below?

CROSSWORD

RUGBY FACTS

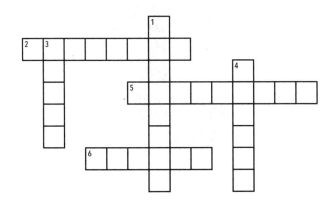

ACROSS

2 Women's national nickname (3,5)

5 Wheelchair rugby known as this in USA (4,5)

6 Scheduled 2023 union World Cup host country (6)

DOWN

1 Former England union captain, Bill ____ (8)

3 Inventor of rugby, William Webb ____ (5)

4 Surname of rugby league legend, found in animal hole perhaps? (6)

TRIVIA
QUOTE COMPLETIONS

Here are two belting quotes from rugby players. We've omitted the end of each quote, so decide which of the three options correctly completes each one.

1. When playing for Harlequins, Joe Marler once asked Kiwi referee Andrew Small, to the amusement of the commentary team, "Are you wearing those boots…"
a) because your wife told you to?
b) tonight at the nightclub?
c) for a bet?

2. On a less then successful campaign, Gareth Davies once quipped, "We've lost seven of our last eight matches. Only team that we've beaten was Western Samoa. Good job we didn't play…"
a) the rest of the world
b) New Zealand on form
c) the whole of Samoa

DOT-TO-DOT

Join the dots to find the mystery image!

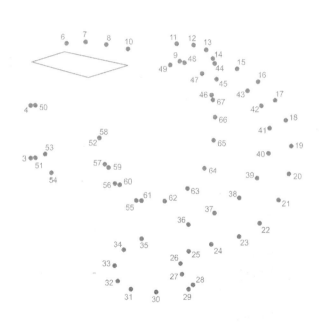

PAIRS GAME

Match up the 20 touch judge flags in 20 seconds. The first one has been done for you.

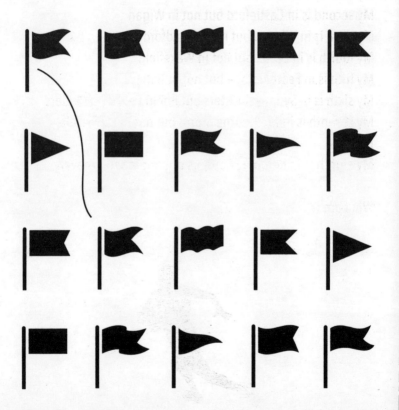

RIDDLE

An attacking rugby move is the answer to this riddle.

My first is in Salford but not in Leigh
My second is in Castleford but not in Wigan
My third is in Widnes but not in Bradford
My fourth is in Leeds but not in Wakefield
My fifth is in Featherstone but not in Batley
My sixth is in Sydney Roosters but not in Canberra Raiders
My seventh is in Melbourne Storm but not in Newcastle Knights
My eighth is in Keighley Cougars but not in Whitehaven

What am I?

CROSSWORD

FAMOUS RUGBY PLAYERS' SURNAMES

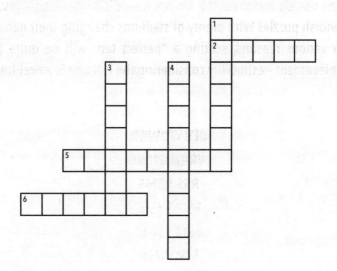

ACROSS

2 Sounds like snake-like fish (5)

5 Siblings fought at this famous battle (8)

6 Meat patty (6)

DOWN

1 18th century war of this ear (7)

3 Add "se" to a European capital (7)

4 Small verdant forest (9)

MISSING VOWELS

The following UK northern rugby league stadiums have had their vowels removed. No, it's not a medical operation – just a fiendish puzzle! With plenty of stadiums changing their names for various reasons, scoring a "perfect ten" will be quite an achievement – especially considering the last one is vowel-free!

CLV WDWRD

WRRN GTLND

RSS RSMS

MCHL CHK

GSLL MTHR

STV HNSN

GRHM HNRY

SMN MDDLTN

N MCGCHN

MRK LFFMN

WORD WHEEL

See how many words of four or more letters you can make from the below letters, using each letter just once. All words must use the central letter. Can you find the name of an item of rugby equipment often used by players?

SPOT THE DIFFERENCE

Can you find the 10 differences between these two pictures?

TRIVIA
NICKNAME ORIGINS

Below are three nicknames of English rugby union players. Which of the options are the correct origins of each nickname?

1. Elliot Daly – "Briefcase"
a) Daly turned up to a training session in school uniform carrying said item
b) As a child, he carried his rugby gear in a briefcase
c) Daly is a trained lawyer so he often carried briefcases around

2. Jonathan Joseph – "ET Fingers"
a) Away from his native Derby, Joseph would often ask his rugby pals for their mobile phones so he could "phone home"
b) Joseph has a knack of carrying a rugby ball one-handed
c) According to his first club coach, Joseph had handling that was "out of this world"

3. Joe Marler – "Croissant"
a) His preferred pre-match energy boost is a buttered croissant
b) While on tour, Marler once got lost in a Parisian bakery
c) His teammates think he has a nose resembling a French pastry

MAZE

Oh no! The game is ready to start, but the touch judge has lost their flag. The spectators are getting restless so, to avoid any more delays, can you help them find their flag?

RUGBY JUMBLE

Six super ladies were shortlisted for the rugby league 2022 Woman of Steel award. Georgia Roche and Amy Hardcastle were two of them; the remaining four players are below – with their surnames cunningly separated and jumbled up. Can you rearrange the groups of letters to reveal the four surnames?

ACH	CU	DD
EY	AM	STA
NN	GH	PE
NL	IN	DO

WORD SEARCH

ENGLISH CLUBS

N	I	S	J	K	E	R	S	L	H	I	R
O	O	B	N	R	L	G	B	N	S	X	E
T	X	D	S	E	A	H	T	A	N	I	T
P	O	B	L	T	E	X	R	Q	T	H	S
M	A	T	B	E	R	A	C	N	S	H	E
A	B	A	M	X	C	T	I	V	C	E	C
H	A	R	L	E	Q	U	I	N	S	K	U
T	O	X	N	L	E	I	F	S	A	L	O
R	G	S	A	H	N	E	B	A	L	T	L
O	R	C	I	J	A	R	A	S	E	B	G
N	R	E	T	S	E	C	I	E	L	O	R

Gloucester, Sale, Harlequins, Northampton, Saracens, Leicester, Exeter, Bath

TRIVIA
A STAR IN THE MAKING!

In late 2021, 10-year-old Arthur Cripps from Cheadle, Greater Manchester, hit the headlines because of an inspiring rugby-related story. Read the following three options and decide which is the correct reason.

a) The Northern youngster was top try scorer in only his second match, which was an Under 15s match. Such is his prestigious talent, he then scored an eye-opening 12 tries in a match the week after.

b) Arthur couldn't play his beloved rugby for health reasons, so he decided to do the second best thing – take up refereeing. The young official went from refereeing school matches to tournaments and, with sound advice from Luke Pearce, his career as a referee looks set to be a successful one.

c) After watching their son play rugby for the first time in a school match, Arthur's parents immediately went to a well-known bookmakers to enquire the odds of Arthur playing for the England national side by the time he turns 20 years of age. A representative of the bookmakers subsequently went to see Arthur in action and reduced the odds by 50%!

FOLLOW THE LETTERS

Starting with any letter, but going from letter to letter either vertically or horizontally, try to find the name of a rugby league superstar. He played his last professional league game for his club in 2015. To give you a helping hand, the starting letter is in the first half of the alphabet!

B	A	C	K	V	E	S
O	T	N	S	I	N	T
H	T	I	H	G	F	O
T	E	V	O	E	I	C
I	K	U	W	L	G	U
P	A	L	F	D	Y	D
G	O	N	O	B	E	N

REBUS

Can you work out who is suggested by the diagram below? He made 27 appearances for his country.

MAZE

Coach Eddie Jones needs to relay some important tactical information to his players during an injury break, but he's misplaced his headset! Can you help him find it in the maze below?

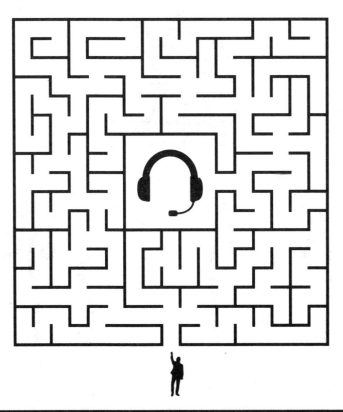

FOR CLUB AND COUNTRY

This requires some obscure knowledge, coupled with intelligent guessing! We've listed 15 rugby union or league clubs from around the world. Try to correctly match the clubs with their country.

DAC KOWLOON	FINLAND
KOALAS RUGBY CLUB	NEW ZEALAND
SALISH ROVERS	CANADA
BOLAND CAVALIERS	ARGENTINA
MERALOMA RUGBY CLUB	PAPUA NEW GUINEA
SALUZZO ROOSTERS	HONG KONG
RC WOMBATS	AUSTRIA
KUOPIO RUGBY CLUB	MEXICO
LA PLATA RUGBY CLUB	ROMANIA
NONDESCRIPTS RF CLUB	SOUTH AFRICA
BULLER RUGBY CLUB	WALES
SAITAMA WHITE KNIGHTS	USA
CSU ALBA IULIA	ITALY
DOWLAIS RFC	JAPAN
LCR JUGGERNAUTS RU CLUB	KENYA

DOT-TO-DOT

Join the dots to find the mystery image!

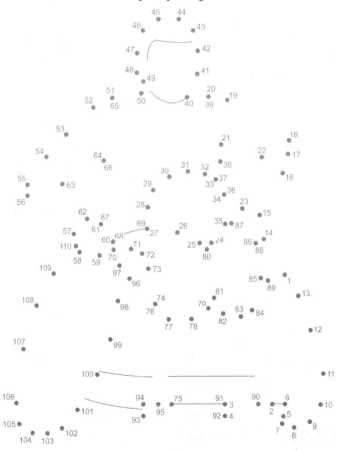

RUGBY JUMBLE

World Rugby named their "Men's 15s Dream Team" in 2021. Four of the union players' surnames have been separated and jumbled up below. Can you work out the surnames by joining them up?

NG   **NT**   **PO**

BA   **GG**   **FU**

RRE   **HO**   **RLO**

DU   **TT**

TRIVIA
1–10

The answers to the following questions are numbers between 1 and 10. Each number can only be used once.

1. In a traditional rugby union team, which number appears in the name of a playing position?
2. The third Rugby Union World Cup was held in 199…?
3. How many tries did David Campese score at the Rugby Union World Cup?
4. How many points are awarded for a drop goal in rugby league?
5. When Wales were knocked out of the 1999 Rugby Union World Cup quarter final by Australia, how many points did they score?
6. In rugby union, the hooker usually plays with which number on the back of their shirt?
7. In rugby league, how many players usually form a scrum?
8. In a game of Rugby Sevens, how many minutes are in each half?
9. As of November 2022, how many times have New Zealand won the men's Rugby Union World Cup?
10. What was the customary number on the back of England legend Martin Johnson's shirt?

"WHO ARE YOU CALLING...?!"

As with several sports, the world of rugby is awash with players' nicknames. Below are some nicknames of professional players – both retired and current. Simply match them up to the correct players to achieve your goal.

FUN BUS	KEITH WOOD
JUDITH	NICK EASTER
THE CHIROPRACTOR	LEWIS MOODY
36	CRAIG CHALMERS
MINTY	IAN MCLAUCHAN
THE RAGING POTATO	BRIAN LIMA
MAD DOG	JASON LEONARD
MIGHTY MOUSE	BILLY TWELVETREES

LETTERBOX

Cross out all the letters below that appear more than once. The remaining letters will then spell out something often seen at rugby matches – whatever the standard! What is it?

B	G	A	O	T
U	M	I	C	E
S	Y	E	H	R
D	Y	F	D	U
R	H	I	M	O
B	G	T	C	N

WORD WHEEL

See how many words of four or more letters you can make from
the below letters, using each letter just once. All words must use
the central letter. Can you find the surname of a Welsh "kicking
machine"?

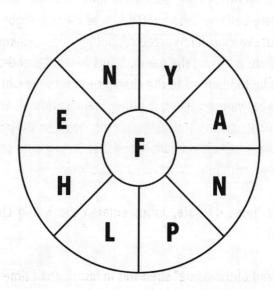

TRIVIA
A STAR IN THE MAKING!

Matty Johns is an Australian ex-rugby league player and media personality. He revealed a now-legendary drinking story that occurred in 2013, after being "on the wagon" for a few months.

In Manly, North Sydney, Johns bumped into the Melbourne coach Craig Bellamy, who invited him to watch a rugby league game that evening. Johns accepted, but not before sinking a few beers. While watching the game, Johns heard the end-of-game siren, so he toddled off to the changing room to see his rugby mates, who were receiving a rather stern telling-off from the coach. Johns commiserated the players on their performance, telling them "it's only a game" and that they should come out on the town with him. What was Johns's mistake?

a) In his "relaxed" state, Johns entered the wrong changing room!

b) The "end-of-the-game" siren was in fact the half-time one!

c) Upon departing the changing room, Johns tripped over a TV cable which meant no one could be interviewed!

WORD SEARCH

ENGLISH WOMEN'S RUGBY LEAGUE PLAYERS

```
B  G  I  G  H  M  D  O  R  I  F  H
L  O  Y  E  L  N  A  T  S  E  H  G
O  L  I  F  G  B  N  R  E  A  H  S
K  D  B  N  R  M  D  C  R  I  J  X
X  T  L  I  A  O  E  D  J  K  M  U
I  H  E  R  D  B  C  X  M  O  I  E
W  O  F  D  L  A  D  H  G  D  X  N
O  R  X  U  S  R  E  V  E  E  B  Y
R  P  D  T  D  B  E  B  R  H  Y  L
V  I  L  B  A  M  O  L  X  U  E  O
S  E  T  A  B  E  K  R  U  B  O  M
```

Stanley, Beevers, Goldthorp, Hardcastle, Burke, Roche, Dodd, Molyneux

WORD LADDER

In this word ladder, change one letter at a time to turn the word
SPIT into FLAG.

SPIT
_ _ _ _
_ _ _ _
_ _ _ _
_ _ _ _
FLAG

TRIVIA
FANS' GREATEST UNION XV

Rugbypass.com is a website dedicated to rugby fans' opinions. It recently published the greatest men's rugby union XV, as voted for by supporters of the great game. Most of the players in the top spot received over 2,000 votes each. We've left out certain players in their usual positions. Guess correctly the players that have been omitted – there is a connection!

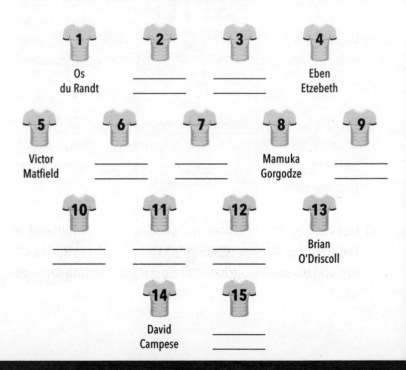

1 Os du Randt

2 _____

3 _____

4 Eben Etzebeth

5 Victor Matfield

6 _____

7 _____

8 Mamuka Gorgodze

9 _____

10 _____

11 _____

12 _____

13 Brian O'Driscoll

14 David Campese

15 _____

TRIVIA
WHERE IS HE NOW?

A lot of sportsmen and -women develop a career in sport after their international days, but others choose a different route. In 2016, ex-England union international Brad Barritt still played for his club Saracens, but decided to sign off his England playing days by doing what?

a) United by his love of coffee, Barritt co-founded the Tiki Tonga coffee company with a friend with a shared love of the roasted beans.

b) Barritt's family persuaded him to regain his passion for long-distance running, which he did with aplomb, even going further by founding an athletic shoe business named Cross Country Elite.

c) Inspired by his penchant for painting, Barritt initiated a business that allows customers (nicknamed "Brad's Buddies") to travel the world sketching the most iconic sporting settings.

PAIRS GAME

Match up the 20 trophies in 20 seconds. The first one has been done for you.

RIDDLE

An illegal rugby move is the answer to this riddle.

My first is in Crusaders but not in Penrith
My second is in Brumbies but not in Blues
My third is in Melrose but not in Hawick
My fourth is in Kelso but not in Gala
My fifth is in Swansea but not in Cardiff
My sixth is in Llanelli but not in Bath
My seventh is in Neath but not in Ulster
My eighth is in Gloucester but not in Saracens

What am I?

ANSWERS

p.6 Trivia
b)

p.7 Word Search:

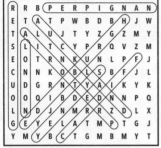

p.8, Crossword
Across: 1 breakdown, 5 turnover, 6 fly half
Down: 2 ankle tap, 3 on the full, 4 Garry Owen

p.9, Pairs Game

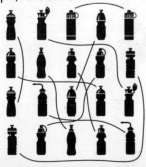

p.10, Trivia
1 Dan Carter, 2 Scotland and England, 3 Toulouse, 4 The Pumas, 5 Scrum-half

p.11, Word Wheel
Word that uses all letters = Whitelock

p.12, Maze

p.13, Anagrams
Lark Davies, Ellie Kildunne, Zoe Harrison, Marlie Packer

p.14, Trivia
c)

p.15, Word Ladder
One possible solution: brow, brew, crew, crow, crop, prop

p.16, Riddle
Dummy

p.17, Dot-to-Dot

p.18, Trivia
b)

p.19, Spot The Difference

p.20, Rebus
Croke Park (it hosted its first ever rugby union match on 11/2/07)

p.21, Missing Vowels
Jonny Wilkinson, Martin Johnson, Brian Moore, Bill Beaumont, Will Carling, Jason Leonard, Rob Andrew, Ellis Genge, Mako Vunipola, Joe Cokanasiga

p.22, Trivia
Men's - Argentina, Japan
Women's - Canada, USA

p.23, Counting Conundrum
ball = 8, boots = 5, whistle = 6, whistle + ball = 14

p.24, Crossword
Across: 2 Chiefs, 5 Tigers, 6 Falcons
Down: 1 Bears, 3 Saints, 4 Sharks

p.25, Anagrams
Campese, Sailor, Underwood, Howlett

p.26, Trivia
15 = Spain, 20 = Portugal

p.27, Riddle
Sevens

p.28, Word Wheel
Word that uses all letters = Wallabies

p.29, Dot-to-Dot

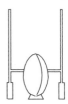

p.30, Spot The Difference

p.31, Missing Letters
21 Chile, 22 Hong Kong, 23 Canada,
24 Namibia, 25 Russia, 26 Belgium,
27 Brazil, 28 Netherlands, 29 Poland,
30 Germany

p.32, Pairs Game

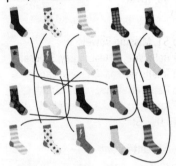

p.33, Word Search

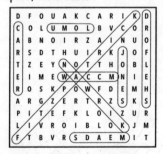

p.34, Trivia
b)

p.35, Letterbox
Bath

p.36, Word Ladder
One possible solution: melt, malt,
salt, sale, bale, ball

p.37, Maze

p.38, Trivia
1 b), 2 a)

p.39, Rugby Jumble
Blood bin, conversion, crash ball,
offload

p.40, Rebus
Hull Kingston Rovers

p.41, Dot-to-Dot

p.42, Trivia
b)

p.43, Anagrams
Clare Daniels, Wayne Barnes,
Jaco Peyper, Luke Pearce

p.44, Word Wheel
Word that uses all letters =
Wakefield

p.45, Pairs Game

p.46, Trivia
1 Diego Dominguez (though he was
born in Argentina!), 2 Murderball,
3, 3 metres, 4 Brian O'Driscoll,
5 Romania, 6 Cape Town,
7 Brian Ashton, 8 New Zealand

p.47, Word Search

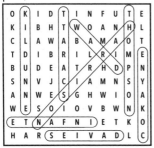

p.48, Letter Grid
Knock on

p.49, Trivia
Australia: 13 Stirling Mortlock,
10 Stephen Larkham, 6 George Smith

England: 15 Josh Lewsey,
12 Mike Tindall, 7 Neil Back

p.50, Trivia
c)

p.51, Missing Vowels
1 Belle Vue, 2 Headingley, 3 Odsal,
4 Totally Wicked, 5 Craven Park,
6 Halliwell Jones, 7 John Smith's,
8 Kingston Park, 9 Cougar Park,
10 DW [Stadium]

p.52, Letterbox
Hanley

p.53, Maze

p.54, Trivia
a)

p.55, Rugby Jumble
North, Tipuric, Faletau, Edwards

p.56, Spot The Difference

p.57, Crossword
Across: 3 Kolbe, 5 Russell, 6 Montoya
Down: 1 Hunter, 2 Barrett, 4 Healey

p.58, Trivia
b)

p.59, Word Search

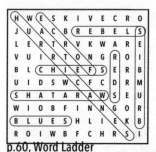

p.60, Word Ladder
One possible solution: boot, book,
cook, rook, rock, ruck

p.61, Rebus
Cauliflower ears

p.62, Trivia
c)

p.63, Dot-to-Dot

p.64, Rebus
Truck and trailer

p.65, Pairs Game

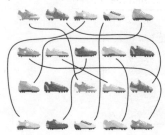

p.66, Trivia
c)

p.67, Word Wheel
Word that uses all letters = goalposts

p.68, Anagram
1 Murrayfield, 2 Eden Park,
3 Twickenham, 4 Ellis Park,

p.69, Riddle
Hooper

p.71, Word Search

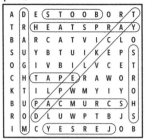

p.72, Rugby Jumble
Calcutta, Bledisloe, Webb Ellis, Lansdowne

p.73, Spot The Difference

p.74, Trivia
b)

p.75, Maze

p.76, Riddle
Offiah

p.77, Crossword
Across: 4 Bulls, 6 Highlanders
Down: 1 Cheetahs, 2 Toulouse, 3 Crusaders, 5 Lazio

p.78, Trivia
1 a), 2 b), 3 b), 4c)

p.79, Follow The Letters
Johnson, Nonu, Umaga, Andrew

p.80, Missing Vowels
1 Sarra Elgan, 2 Jonathan Davies, 3 Maggie Alphonsi, 4 Dylan Hartley, 5 Stuart Hogg, 6 Sean Fitzpatrick, 7 Michael Lynagh, 8 Bryan Habana, 9 Alan Quinlan, 10 Jamie Roberts

p.81, Word Ladder
Onc possible solution: pope, pole, pale, male, mall, maul

p.82, Trivia
1 b), 2 a), 3 c)

p.83, Letterbox
France

p.84, Rebus
Forward pass

p.85, Trivia
1 = 1897, 2 = 2003, 3 = 1888, 4 = 1995, 5 = 1871, 6 = 1987,

7 = 1977, 8 = 1871, 9 = 1917,
10 = 1883, 11 = 1900

p.86, Word Search

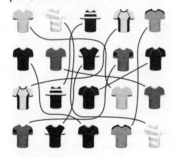

p.87, Pairs Game

p.88, Word Wheel
Words that use all letters =
Scrum half ("9" was the clue!)

p.89, Crossword
Across: 4 Red Devils, 5 Dragons,
6 Giants
Down: 1 Rhinos, 2 Warriors,
3 Wolves

p.90, Trivia
1 c), 2 b), 3 b)

p.91, Dot-to-Dot

p.92, Spot The Difference

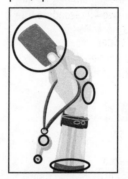

p.93, Anagrams
Scrum machine, shoulder pads,
tackle bag, water bottle

p.94, Trivia
1 c), 2 c), 3 b)

p.95, Rugby Jumble
Burgess, Makinson, Watkins,
Bateman

p.96, Odd One Out
3. Joe Marler - he's the only forward
in the list. The others (Jonah Lomu,

Dan Carter, Tim Horan, Rob Howley, Shane Williams and Serge Blanco) were all backs

p.97, Riddle
Grubber

p.98, Trivia
1 false - Canada, 2 true, 3 true,
4 false - only the captain may do this,
5 false - they have 40 seconds, 6 true

p.99, Word Ladder
One possible solution: loft, lift, list, last, past, pass

p.100, Rebus
Goosestep (made famous by David Campese)

p.101, Crossword
Across: 2 Red Roses, 5 Quad rugby, 6 France
Down: 1 Beaumont, 3 Ellis, 4 Burrow

p.102, Trivia
1 c), 2 c)

p.103, Dot-to-Dot

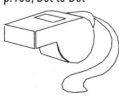

p.104, Pairs Game

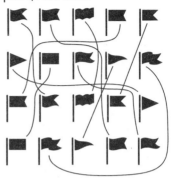

p.105, Riddle
Scissors

p.106, Crossword
Across: 2 Eales, 5 Hastings, 6 Burger
Down: 1 Jenkins, 3 Parisse, 4 Greenwood

p.107, Missing Vowels
1 Clive Woodward, 2 Warren Gatland,
3 Rassie Erasmus, 4 Michael Cheika,
5 Giselle Mather, 6 Steve Hansen,
7 Graham Henry, 8 Simon Middleton,
9 Ian McGeechan, 10 Mark Luffman

p.108, Word Wheel
Word that uses all letters = Headguard

p.109, Spot The Difference

p.110, Trivia
1 a), 2 b), 3 c)

p.111, Maze

p.112, Rugby Jumble
Peach, Cunningham, Dodd, Stanley

p.113, Word Search

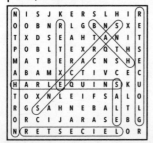

p.114, Trivia
b)

p.115, Follow The Letters
Kevin Sinfield

p.116, Rebus
Tony Underwood

p.117, Maze

p.118, For Club and Country
1 = 6,	2 = 8,	3 = 12,
4 = 10,	5 = 3,	6 = 13,
7 = 7,	8 = 1,	9 = 4,
10 = 15,	11 = 2,	12 = 14,
13 = 9,	14 = 11,	15 = 5

p.119, Dot-to-Dot

Dupont, Hogg, Barrett, Furlong

p.121, Trivia
1 = 8, 2 = 5, 3 = 10, 4 = 1, 5 = 9,
6 = 2, 7 = 6, 8 = 7, 9 = 3, 10 = 4

p.122, "Who're You Calling…?!"
1 = 7, 2 = 4, 3 = 6, 4 = 8,
5 = 2, 6 = 1, 7 = 3, 8 = 5

p.123, Letterbox
Fans

p.124, Word Wheel
Word that uses all letters =
Halfpenny

p.125, Trivia
b)

p.126, Word Search
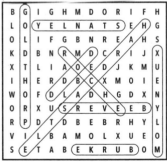

p.127, Word Ladder
One possible solution: spit, slit, slip,
slap, flap, flag

p.128, Trivia
2 = Sean Fitzpatrick, 3 = Owen Franks,
6 = Jerome Kaino, 7 = Richie McCaw,
9 = Aaron Smith, 10 = Dan Carter,
11 = Jonah Lomu, 12 = Ma'a Nonu,
15 = Christian Cullen.
They are all New Zealanders.

p.129, Trivia
a)

p.130, Pairs Game

p.131, Riddle
crossing

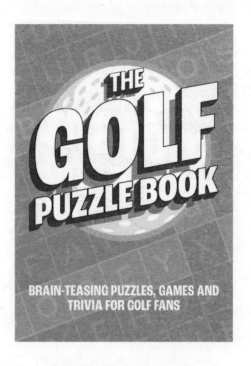

The Golf Puzzle Book

Paperback

978-1-80007-920-5

Discover word searches, riddles, crosswords, spot the differences and much more in this fun-filled activity book for golf lovers. Whether you're trying to match the pairs of golf clubs or helping putt the ball through the maze, this book is guaranteed to be a favourite for all who enjoy the game.

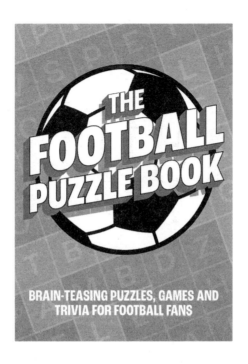

The Football Puzzle Book

Paperback

978-1-80007-921-2

Discover word searches, riddles, crosswords, spot the differences and much more in this fun-filled activity book for football lovers. Whether you're diving through a maze to make an incredible save or trying to match the pairs of football boots, this book is guaranteed to be a favourite for all who e njoy the game.

Have you enjoyed this book?

If so, find us on Facebook at
Summersdale Publishers, on Twitter at
@Summersdale and on Instagram and TikTok at
@summersdalebooks and get in touch.

We'd love to hear from you!

www.summersdale.com

Image credits

Cover design by Ric Gray; Cover image © Christiaan Lloyd/Shutterstock.com;
Player p.5 and throughout © Nebojsa Kontic/Shutterstock.com; Socks p.9 © Aleksey
Zhuravlev/Shutterstock.com; Player p.10 and throughout © MurzillA/Shutterstock.
com; Whistle p.12 and throughout © Fox Design/Shutterstock.com; Umpire p.12 ©
Miceking/Shutterstock.com; Puzzle p.17 © Pavel K/Shutterstock.com; Puzzle p.19
© GSapphire/Shutterstock.com; Frog p.20 © lineartestpilot/Shutterstock.com; Park
icon © Nadiinko/Shutterstock.com; Shoes p.23 © Pavel K/Shutterstock.com; Puzzle
p.29 © Yevgen Lagunov/Shutterstock.com; Puzzle p.30 © xamyak/Shutterstock.com;
Bottles p.32 © Alexkava/Shutterstock.com; Tee p.37 © Jiripravda/Shutterstock.com;
King p.40 © Vectorfair/Shutterstock.com; UK p.40 © Kolia_stock/Shutterstock.com;
Rover p.40 © Ctrl-x/Shutterstock.com; Puzzle p.41 © brichuas/Shutterstock.com;
First Aid Kit p.53 © Luckyest/Shutterstock.com; Spray p.53 © pnDl/Shutterstock.
com; Puzzle p.56 © Excess/Shutterstock.com; Collie p.61 © A7880S/Shutterstock.
com; Wheat p.61 © ysclips design/Shutterstock.com; Flower p.61 © Hasebalcon/
Shutterstock.com; Puzzle p.63 © Michal Sanca/Shutterstock.com; Truck p.64 ©
Line – design/Shutterstock.com; Trailer p.64 © Far700/Shutterstock.com; Shoes
p.65 © Anatolir/Shutterstock.com; Puzzle p.73 © Elena Istomina/Shutterstock.com;
Beer p.75 © Gamegfx/Shutterstock.com; Clock p.84 © Ahmad Muflih Syarifuddin/
Shutterstock.com; Ward and pass p.84 © bsd studio/Shutterstock.com; T-Shirt
p.87 © Gareth Lent/Shutterstock.com; Puzzle p.91 © Prayuda/Shutterstock.com;
Puzzle p.92 © Dmytro Nychytalyuk/Shutterstock.com; Foot p.100 © PPVector/
Shutterstock.com; Goose p.100 © barka/Shutterstock.com; Puzzle p.103 © Ray
Senlye/Shutterstock.com; Flags pp. 104, 111 © WarmWorld/Shutterstock.com;
Puzzle p.109 © xamyak/Shutterstock.com; Umpire p.111 © Snap2Art/Shutterstock.
com; Tree p.116 © SurfsUp/Shutterstock.com; Knee p.116 © AVIcon/Shutterstock.
com; Toe p.116 © howcolour/Shutterstock.com; Umpire p.117 © NadzeyaShanchuk/
Shutterstock.com; Headset p.117 © FARBAI/Shutterstock.com; Puzzle p.119 ©
Simple Line/Shutterstock.com; Trophies p.130 © ksenvitaln/Shutterstock.com